# Gardens Flowers

# Gardens Flowers

*Engraving by Dürer, Redouté, Daffinger and several artists*

## Texts by Matthias Hermann

*Translated by Grace Jackman*

## Minerva

Flowers are the delight of the earth; they deck it out in all seasons with delicate garlands whose shapes and shades are continually being renewed. They are also the joy and consolation of men; they offer us a feast of color, their heady perfume; even when dead, they have the gift of healing many sufferings.

"Happy are those who love flowers," Alphonse Karr used to say who was patron of the horticulturists of Nice, and he liked to add "Happy are those who love only flowers." This second postulation is a little too exclusive; however, loving only flowers would be one sure way of avoiding the disillusion and pain invariably found in human affections!

In any case, it is easy to understand those who surround themselves with flowers, cultivate them, and have a predilection for gardens where they reign supreme.

# The Hundred Flowers *(Chinese Tale)*

In the reign of Yin-Tsang there lived in the small village of Tchang-Yo, a farmer's son who had a few acres of land around his small house. Although his name was Tsieou-Sien, he was scarcely ever called anything other than Hoa-Tchy (the flower maniac).

He did in fact have a mad passion for flowers: in a very short time his garden had become a thing of wonder; all the most beautiful and rare flowers grew there at will; since he loved them well, Hoa-Tchy knew how to look after them.

However many plants he had, he visited them one by one, treating them like children, full of solicitude at all times, touching in his attentions, his gentle care.

When mud had dirtied a petal, he would wash it with clear water, calling this *the bathing of the flowers.*

If one of them had been torn up by the wind or cut by some scoundrel he would bind the wound and hence this was called *the healing of the flowers.*

When the bad season came carrying off his tender charges, Hoa-Tchy would sob in distress to see them wither. He would pick up the fallen flowers, gather them into vases and put them in the earth; he called this ceremony *the burial of the flowers.*

Hoa-Tchy's garden was so remarkable that he became a celebrity throughout the country like his owner who was called Tsieou-Kong (Mr. Tsieou); he himself was known as "the old man who loves his garden."

He lived happy amidst his dear flowers, but alas one fine day a ne'er-do-well came to settle not far from his home—one Tchang-Oey, a mandarin's son, banished by his father because of his debauchery—and brought with him a company of swaggerers like himself.

5

One day, on leaving an orgy with his companions, he passed Tsieou's garden which was then bright with the rarest peonies: the "green butterfly," the "great red lion," the "sparkling blue lion" vied with each other in striking beauty; the libertine wanted to force his way in. Since the old man opposed him, Tchang-Oey threatened him: "Do you not know who I am, old man? The whole town knows me: my name is Tchang-Nonouy (Tchang from within the Palace) and you will pay dearly for any resistance. I want to pick the flowers and I shall do so."

"My Lord, strike down the old Chinese, kill him, torture him, but as long as there is breath in his body you will not touch his flowers!"

"Talkative nuisance, you'll see," cried the prince, and signalling to his companions, he began ruthlessly tearing up the peonies, pulling of their leaves and buds.

"Arrant knaves, rogues and rascals," shrieked the old man sobbing as he saw the petals strewn about on the ground... In a sudden fury, he fell with fists flying on Tchang-Oey; the latter being three parts drunk and unsteady on his feet, stumbled under the old man's rush. Indeed the old man might have been struck down by the prince's friend had not one of them— who was less drunk than the others, older and more reasonable—fearing some serious mischief, managed to calm the over-excited band...

Tsieou-Sien could not leave his dead flowers; bent over them he sobbed, "Oh flowers, that I loved so much and ceaselessly protected throughout my life, I would have trembled at the very idea of touching the most delicate of your petals!

"And now you weep in disorder; you are like a purple cloud!

"My pretty flowers, your life is ended; you lie as if beaten down by tempest and hail!"

"Why are you crying thus, poor Tsieou-Sien, why do you despair?" said a gentle voice suddenly in the old man's ear.

He turned around. A young girl barely sixteen years old, simply dressed and wonderfully beautiful, stood behind him.

"Who are you and why have you come into my garden that has been laid waste?" said Tsieou trembling.

"I am your neighbor and I want to admire your peonies in flower."

The poor Chinese broke into sobs and told his tale of misfortune.

"And that is why you are so sad? If you like I can give your flowers back their life and their beauty."

"Why do you make fun of the poor Chinese? A flower torn from its stem cannot be restored any more than the severed head of an executed man."

"Do not be sure", said the young girl. "My ancestors gave me the secret of this miracle. Go and fetch me some water."

Stupefied, the old man knelt down before her and then rose to do her bidding; but half

way there he hesitated, turned round and cried out in astonishment.

The young girl had disappeared but all the flowers and leaves that had been strewn about on the ground were back on their stems, and they were more wonderful than ever; the singles had become doubles, the plain colors had become variegated. Every head had at the same time the colors of all the varieties, colors that were one hundred times brighter than before.

Tsieou's neighbors soon learnt of this miracle and came crowding to the gates of his garden, but knowing how strange the owner was they did not dare go in.

Tsieou was a man of great good sense. He thought about the strange events that had happened.

"It is because I always sincerely loved my flowers that the gods who care for them came to my aid, but it is because I jealously guarded for me alone the sight of all these treasures that heaven has punished me. I know today that immortals are protecting me, they who have unlimited power and goodness, so I shall no longer close my garden to the curious."

What great amazement there was when the old man opened his gate to everyone!

However, the mandarin's son, furious at having been beaten, called together his companions and told them: "Yesterday this old scoundrel knocked me over: I want vengeance. Let us go to his garden and destroy it completely; there will be not one flower left standing on its stem, not one bud in its calyx, not one leaf on its stalk! Let us tear up and burn everything!"

And they all set out for Tsieou's house.

On the way, they learnt of the miracle of day before: "Ha, ha!" sniggered the prince. "That old madman has the power to call down the gods? That's a lot of nonsense; a false rumor that he spreading to stop us from going into his place!"

But when they got there and saw the gates of the garden standing open and the paths full of people admiring the resuscitated flowers, they had to accept the proof.

"Let us leave this garden", said Tchang, "I have another plan: at the moment anyone who has dealings with witchcraft is being tried and condemned to terrible tortures. Let us denounce this old dog Tsieou, and his enchanted garden will be mine."

The plan was put into action. Tsieou was arrested. "What crime has the old Chinese committed?" He cried when they put the garrotte on him.

But unheeding, they heaped insult on him, calling him an old witch, a bandit, and under good escort took him off to prison.

"Alas!" lamented the poor old man stretched out on the straw, the cangue round his neck: "It is because a young immortal girl gave my flowers back their life that they are going to torture me! Oh, goddess, if old Tsieou can still inspire some pity in you, come to his aid."

He had scarcely uttered this prayer when the young girl appeared. The cangue fell from the prisoner's neck and his irons from his limbs.

"Oh, powerful immortal, tell me your name that I may venerate it for ever."

7

"I am the guardian spirit of gardens. Our Queen felt pity for you and because of your goodness the spirit that protects flowers told the ruler of the sky; your persecutors will be punished and you in a few years will obtain your reward. Your compassion for flowers has won you merit in our eyes. Eat only flowers henceforward and you will come to the perfection that makes man immortal."

The old gardener was found guilty of witchcraft. But when the executioners fell on him to clamp his limbs into instruments of torture, the judge, suddenly dizzy, fell into a faint, and execution was stayed.

Meanwhile, preceded by the servants who had been ordered to prepare a banquet, the mandarin's son and his accomplices had gone to the enchanted garden.

They were rolling about drunk in the flowerbeds, when a whirlwind arose; under its violent blast all the flowers stood up and turned into young girls in robes as bright as the petals of the most beautiful corollas.

One of them spoke. "We are all sisters of the flowers; the enemies of Tsieou who has always protected us are our enemies, so let us unite our efforts to combat them."

And waving their wide sleeves to and fro they thus produced a dreadful storm.

The prince and his companions fled in terror.

The sky was pitch black: nothing could be discerned.

And the rogues went stumbling into the trees, hurt themselves on the branches, tore themselves on the thorns while running away. Tchang, in a panic, fell into the dung-pit where he choked and died.

The next day, when the Supreme Court judge learned what had happened, he was overcome with fear: after the warning of the fainting-spell the previous day, and knowing quite well in any case that the old Chinese had been unjustly condemned, he gave orders to set him free and gave him a decree bearing his seal to say no-one should dare to touch the humblest flower in Tsieou's garden.

From that moment onwards, the good gardener lived happy and at peace among his beloved plants.

He ate only fallen flowers, and strange to tell, his white hair became black again, his lines disappeared and his face became fresh as in very early youth.

One day when he was sitting in his garden, looking lovingly at a newly-opened peony, a gentle breeze caressed him bearing exquisite melodies and piercing-sweet perfumes hitherto unknown.

A young goddess, preceded by pure white storks and an azure phoenix came down towards him on a cloud:

"Tsieou-Sien, you have attained perfect merit. The master of the sky wishes to reward your love for flowers and calls you to his celestial gardens. Follow me..."

Tsieou stepped on to the cloud and was slowly raised toward the sky.

His hut, trees and plants, everything he held dear, rose with him.

And from the cloud came a voice which said,

"He who loves flowers and protects them has greater happiness and will know every kind of joy!

He who illtreats them or destroys them will be unhappy and will know the harshest punishments!"

The cloud was lost among other clouds, and the only sound to be heard was the gentle murmuring of the breeze.

Tsieou's village changed its name to that of Ching-Sien-Li (village of the immortal raised to the sky). It is also called "village of the hundred flowers."

# The Flower

In ordinary language, the word *flower* is used to mean the brightest part of a plant, and hence we say that some plants do not have *flowers*. For the botanist, the *flower* is the organ or rather the set of organs essential for reproduction. All these organs are modifications, or changes in the leaf. All the intermediate stages can be found in floral leaves or bracts. The *flower* may be regarded, then, as a compressed shoot held up by a special support commonly called a *stem* in scientific language the *peduncle*. When this flower stalk is so short that it seems to be completely missing, the *flower* is called *sessile*. When it branches, the primary axis is called the peduncle and the flower-bearing branches are called *pedicels*. The *scape* is the word used for all the flower stalks arising from a bulb or a rosette of radical leaves, and that are bare or have only a few bracts. The arrangement of the flowers on the stalks bears the name of *inflorescence*. The same name is given to a set of flowers that are not separated one from the other by leaves as such.

A flower, regarded as a whole, is made up of several verticils of differently modified leaves. The external verticil(s) which are protective organs are called *floral envelopes* or *perianth* or *perigone.* This term in a more particular sense is applied to the floral envelope of mono-cotyledons, that is almost always single, or at least made up of more or less similar parts as

in the hyacinth, the lily, the tulip, etc.   When the perianth is double, which happens in most
of the dicotyledons, the external envelope takes the name of *calyx* and the internal one that
of *corolla.*   The first is usually like a leaf in terms of texture and color; the second is of
more fragile tissue and the colors are more varied and often brighter.   Take for example the
camelia, wallflower, pink, rose, etc.   Sometimes, however, the calyx is coloured or *petaloid*
as in the wallflower.   This happens particularly whenever the corolla is missing as in clematis,
hellebore, Marvel of Peru, and birthwort.   Inside the floral envelope are the sex organs which
are the most important part of the flower, i.e the *androecium,* a set of *stamens* or male organs
and in the centre the *gynaeceum* which is the set of pistils or female organs.   At the bottom
of many flowers, there are special organs called *nectaries* of a glandular type but fairly varied
in shape.   The component parts of the different verticils are arranged in such a way that the
members of one whorl or verticil are placed opposite the intervals between the members of the
next whorl because of the great law of the alternation of verticils; exceptions to this law are
rare; often they are exceptions in appearance only.

Before being completely blown and when still in the bud stage, the various component parts
of the flower and particularly those of the two external verticils are curled up or folded over
themselves like leaves in buds; this arrangement is the *aestivation* or *prefloration.*   Each verticil
is made up of a fairly variable number of parts; but very often the numbers 3, 5 and their
multiples are found.   The first is the *ternary* type found in monocotyledons; the second the
*pentamerous* type found only in dicotyledons.   But these types may be altered by doubling
(chorisis), modifications, non-formation (abortion), etc.   Complete *flowers* are those with a
calyx and a corolla; *apetalous* flowers are those that have only the first of these two envelopes;
naked or achlamydeous if they have neither calyx nor corolla.   A distinction is made between
hermaphrodite or monoclinous *flowers* which have both stamens and pistils (this is the more
usual); *unisexual* or *diclinous,* those that have organs of only one sex; *male* flowers have
only stamens; *female* flowers have only pistils; *neuter* have none at all. Monoecious plants
are those that have male and female flowers on the same plant, like the oak; dioecious those
that have male flowers on one plant and female flowers on another, like the willow; *polygamous*
those that have on the same plant or on different plants male, female and hermaphrodite flowers,
like the ash.   The verticils of a given flower may sometimes stick together.   The various parts
of the same verticil may develop unevenly which makes for irregularity in the flowers.   A distinction must be made between *regular* and *symmetrical flowers.*   The first, like the rose or
bellflower, may be divided into two equal parts by a straight line drawn through the center in
any direction; the second, like the snapdragon or sweetpea, can be divided in this way in one
direction only.   Almost all irregular flowers are symmetrical; those that are neither regular nor
symmetrical are very rare.

The various parts of the flower can undergo changes varying considerably in degree. *Double flowers* are those which have a larger number of petals than is usual, or rather those where the perianth has developed much more than normal. This may be due to various causes. Sometimes the corolla divides into two, as in bellflowers or thorn-apple; sometimes the petaloid appendages, of the axis develop, as in pinks, convolvulus, campion, etc. In composite flowers such as chrysanthemums, dahlias, china asters, the florets in the center change into either ligules or long colored tubes armed with fertile or petaloid stamens. The most usual cause of the doubling of flowers is that stamens change into petals; this is found in roses, delphiniums, hollyhocks or rose-mallows, anemones and buttercups, etc. Double flowers or rather *semidoubles* can give seed. This is not so of *full doubles* where sex organs have been changed into petals; they are always neuter and sterile.

The phenomena that can be observed when a flower opens are called *anthesis, florescence* or *flowering.* The time that this happens varies according to the nature of the species and also to the season of the year or even hour of the day. It can be modified by atmospheric conditions, light, heat, humidity, etc. The lasting quality of flowers is also very variable. While some may last several weeks, there are others with a very short life that bloom and die in the same day; they are called *ephemeral.*

Flowers vary a great deal as to size; those of corn-salad or forget-me-nots are microscopic, while those of Victoria Regina (Royal Water-Lily) may be as much as one metre round. Flower size in any case bears no relation to that of the plant. The oak has flowers that can only be seen with a magnifying glass; the dwarf gentian, which grows to no more than one decimetre has a flower of almost 0.05 m; one species of birthwort has a calyx large enough to use as a hat. The size of the flowers also varies in the same species according to the conditions under which the plant are lived. Generally speaking it can be said that the more flowers there are, the smaller they are.

Flowers vary so much in color that this characteristic is in general of little importance. However there are groups which in this respect have some consistency, which exclude one or another color. Almost all of the umbelliferae have white or yellow flowers; petals on dicotyledons are usually greenish. This characteristic naturally becomes more consistent in smaller groups, for example according to genus. To give only one exception, however, the genus "linum", flax, has blue, white, yellow, pink, red or grey flowers. Cultivation has a certain influence in this respect. Ornamental plants often within the same species have very different or highly variegated shades. White flowers usually predominate in cold regions; white and yellow in temperate regions; red and blue in the equatorial zones. Green or black flowers are very rare.

# Gardens

Flowers must have attracted man's attention from very early times, and he seems to have taken pleasure in gathering them round his home to enjoy at leisure. First he grew those found in the neighborhood, the gradually those that came from further and further afield. To cultivate flowers you need fairly low-lying ground, on the level or on a gentle slope, a good airy place open to light and heat but protected from the cold north winds. There must be a variety of aspects however so that every plant can have the position it requires. The soil must be fertile and well prepared.

Flower cultivation involves several stages of work and needs a lot of care; the amateur is well rewarded for his pains. A flower garden can be laid out according to local conditions and also according to the taste and imagination of the owner. Flowerbeds can take the form of borders, can have straight parallel or curved edges. These flowerbeds should be at most 2 m. wide and can be framed by planks or bricks, or by hardy or annual plants.

It is very useful to have water close by. But the most important thing is the composition of the soil: every plant has special needs in this respect and one corner of the garden must be kept for mixing the earth, which is prepared two years in advance and has to be stirred at least four times a year for its various constituents to be properly combined.

A flower garden must also have forcing beds and frames for bringing on plants, and a place free from frost and damp for storing the bulbs, roots and tubers that do not lie out all year; a variety of tools and implements are needed for flower-growing, in particular an assortment of pots and boxes of various sizes for the plants brought into the hothouse or greenhouse during the winter, or for those that are displayed to their full effect only on staging.

"Staging," said a specialist, „means a kind of wooden staircase usually dismantled during the winter, but otherwise placed against the wall of the house, or a little way off, that holds potted plants when in flower so that the display changes almost every fortnight. Often the plants on the staging are covered during the hottest part of the day by a kind of tent or movable curtain which screens them from the sun thus preserving the flowers longer. Flower-beds of tulips, hyacinths, buttercups, anemones and other plants rarely grown in pots are covered in the same way. The awnings are taken off or folded back in the evening and must be left far enough away from the flowers to allow the air to circulate freely."

The flower garden needs to be kept spotlessly clean; indeed, a little primping is not excessive. The Dutch are past masters in this art; nowhere will you see more carefully raked paths, better trimmed borders, or better pruned shrubs. Everywhere else, landscape gardens

have become the fashion, but in the Netherlands, flower gardens have stayed in favor and you can still see any of the types of garden described below.

The garden with general or mixed flowers offers a mixture of all kinds of flowers arranged so that they mutually enhance each other and follow one another throughout the season. This is the most common type of garden and the type which suits most amateurs; plants with spreading heads ans showy flowers are used. However, a wise choice of species and varieties is much more important than sheer weight of numbers. A gardener of taste can with a few well-chosen elements create variety in the combinations.

The garden with selected or specimen flowers is one where only a few types of plants are used, sometimes indeed only one at a time; these are amateur's or collector's flowers such as anemones, hyacinths, pinks, tulips, annuals—such as chrysanthemums, china asters, larkspurs and exotic flowers—bulbous plants and so on.

The garden with replacement or seasonal flowers has only plants grown in pots, raised in a special place and easily renewable. As soon as the flowers begin to appear, the pots are buried in the flowerbeds, and as soon as they wilt, they are removed and replaced by fresh ones. This is the best way of using all the possibilities of a flowerbed, but it requires a lot of space. The Chinese made excellent use of this method in their famous gardens. They excell in the art of border settings; they prefer flowers that are long-lasting, full, offering beauty of shape and elegance of foliage, and shades that blend with their surroundings.

*Althaea*

# Hollyhock

These are fine large plants, biennials or perennials; the stem grows to some 2 meters and stands erect, bearing broad hairy five-lobed leaves, terminating in a long spike of large flowers, which, according to the variety, can be white, yellow, red, brown, purple or violet.

It is generally believed that hollyhocks were brought back from the Crusades, originating in Syria. They need a light, substantial soil and a southern exposure; they can be sown outdoors, but need frequent watering.

The marsh mallow (althaea officinalis) was used a vegetable in Roman times and has also served as a medicinal plant in the past.

# Anemone

Anemones are herbaceous perennial plants with radical leaves from the middle of which arises a scape carrying a solitary flower. They grow in woods, open meadows, or at the waterside.

The snowdrop anemone is a very common pretty plant; wood-ginger differs from it only by its flowers, which are a beautiful yellow: hence the common name yellow wood anemone.

The florist's anemone seems to have been brought from the East. By cultivation it has produced more than three hundred varieties of doubles, with different colors, shades and shapes.

*Antirrhinum*

# Snapdragon

The characteristics of the antirrhinum are a five-lobed calyx; an irregular corolla, with a large splayed tube, containing a sac-like swelling at the base which is strongly two-lipped, in the form of a mouth; four stamens; a two-celled capsule opened at the apex by three pores. The main species is the *antirrhinum* majus or snapdragon, commonly known as dragon's mouth or lion's mouth, with many regional variations; it is a perennial plants grown in gardens, with single or branched erect stems, dark-green, oblong or lance-shaped leaves (the lower ones arranged opposite one another on either side of the stem, the higher ones alternating with one another) with large pink, purplish or white flowers arranged in clusters.

Snapdragons grow in rocks and old walls, and flower from June to September.

*Aquilegia*

# Columbine

A calyx with five sepals extending by their lower extremity into so many spurs; a large number of stamens; five pistils that become so many follicles: such are the characteristics which put the columbine in the family of the crowfoot. There is some dispute as to the origin of the Latin name *Aquilegia.* Some consider that the words means urn (*aquilegium,* water reservoir) because of the shape of the petals; others trace it from the resemblance of the spurs to the beak and talons of an eagle (*aquila,* eagle).

Whatever the case may be, there are thirteen species of columbine, seven of which are indigenous to Siberia. All are herbaceous perennials.

The common columbine is found in gardens where it shines by the beauty of the blue, red, violet or white flowers, according to the varieties and by its deeply toothed foliage, of a gentle green which later darkens. It likes shade but cannot stand a lot of damp. Its various parts were long thought to have diuretic and antiscorbutic properties; modern medicine has made no use of it.

# Cuckoo-pint

There is a fairly large number of species of arum. The most well known is the cuckoo-pint, variously called wake-robin, lords and ladies or Portland starch root. It is a perennial plant with fibrous roots, from which arise radical leaves on long leaf-stalks of a beautiful green with black spots. The flowers unite to form a spadix borne on a greenish white scape. The fruits are small bright red berries about the size of a pea, uniting to form a sort of tight spike. This plant grows in damp shady places, on the edge of woods, along hedgerows, in fertile land. It flowers early in the spring.

The rhizome (commonly called root) is tuberculous, fleshy, mostly made up of starch; when fresh it has an acrid milky juice that is very caustic. If you bite a lump of this rhizome, your mouth will feel as if it is on fire; it could be serious if this substance reached the stomach. There are countless examples of children being poisoned by eating it.

The starch extract of this root can be put to industrial use; it is used to make gum, finishings, cosmetic pastes and powders; it is even said to soften, whiten and give sheen to the skin. It can therefore in this respect replace the starch extracted from cereals or potatoes. The rhizome can be used as soap; it froths when crushed in water.

# Aster

The aster got its name from the elegantly radiated flowers that look like stars. The most common species, known as the michaelmas daisy, is a downy perennial plant with a creeping root, an erect stem—leaves all along it, single at the bottom, branched at the top with entire or wavy-edged toothed leaves, with flower-heads arranged in a terminal corymb with yellow disc-florets and blueish lilac ray-florets. It is a very pretty plant that grows spontaneously in the woodland and dry slopes in several regions and that is also cultivated in gardens for its pleasing effect.

# Begonia, elephant's ear

Begonias originated in the tropical parts of Asia and America. There is a very large number of species, all outstanding because of the elegant habit of the plant and the pretty white, red or pink flowers often arranged in dichotomies—alternate leaves of various colors, with palmate veins, two large stipules usually divided into two very unequal halves. Begonias are widely cultivated in gardens.

One variety, which came from China, has stalks tinged with red above every articulation; the leaves are green above and deep red below. This species loses its stems in autumn and grows them again in springtime; its tubers withstand the rigors of any winter.

Another variety, originating in Mexico, is a plant with a thick, winding, inclined stem and large oval leaves, heart-shaped, accompanied by reddish appendages covering the veins and encircling the petioles like a cuff; the flowers are white growing in panicles.

Besides the natural species, every year a certain number of varieties and sub-varieties are found, forming the class of hybrid begonias, superior, by the brightness and rich markings of their leaves, to the species from which they came.

*Calendula*

# Marigold

There are more than thirty species of marigold (botanists call it calendula from the Latin *calendae,* which means the first day of the month, because the flowers are renewed every month even during winter when the cold is not too harsh). When grown in gardens it is an annual although it originated in Mediterranean Europe where it grows in fields and vineyards. It has solitary and very bright orange-yellow flowerheads. It needs a light soil and warm exposure.

*Callistephus*

# China aster

Imported into Europe from China around 1730, the China aster soon became one of the most popular garden flowers. It has produced a considerable number of varieties, characterized either by the very habit of the plant and the vegetative organs (large or pyramidal, giant and dwarf, etc.), or by the shape and arrangement of the floral organs, or the color (plain, variegated, etc.). Today only the double or full varieties are appreciated.

*Caltha Palustris*

# Marsh marigold

Marsh marigolds are perennial herbaceous plants. Quite a lot of species are particularly found in the temperate regions of the northern hemisphere. They generally grow in shady, damp or even flooded places. They have the usual properties of the ranunculaceae but to a very high degree. Their beautiful foliage and flowers, generally very early, make them highly suitable for decorating ornamental lakes in parks and gardens.

The common marsh marigold, american cowslip or water buttercup is a stocky plant which grows to a height of 0.35 m; its thick stems bear large rounded crenelated bright green leaves, ending in large, wide open, golden-yellow flowers. It is widely found in the whole of Europe, in Siberia and North America. It flowers from March onwards.

The stem and flowers of marsh marigolds are extremely pungent. The noxious properties reach maximum intensity when the plant is in flower. Its stimulant properties have encouraged its use as an detergent and solvent; but this has more less disappeared.

*Campanula*
# Bellflower

Bellflowers are plants with alternate leaves, generally growing in temperate regions with a preference for mountainous country. Their flowers, arranged in various ways, have an ovoid five-lobed calyx, five stamens, an ovary and above it a style with several longitudinal rows of hair. There are more than 180 species of bellflowers.

Take for example the rampion (peach bells, peach-leaved bellflower), a pretty perennial and hardy plant which grows in the woods. It is cultivated as an ornamental plant and can be eaten as a salad; the large white or blue flowers are striking in flower beds. There is one variety with a calyx modified into a kind of corolla.

All the bellflowers can be grown outside, by sowing their seeds shortly after maturity. Most of them do not come up if you wait for spring to come around again. They should be sown in a light substantial soil.

*Cheiranthus*

# Wallflower

Grown in gardens for the attractive, scented flowers, wallflowers are herbaceous plants with oblong leaves, with very variously colored flowers, which grow in lax terminal clusters. There are about fifteen species, widespread in the temperate and cold regions of the northern hemisphere. They have, to a slight extent the general properties of the cruciferae. The most well-known is the common wallflower or yellow gilliflower which has very sweetly scented beautiful golden-yellow flowers. This plant forms clumps of about 0.35 m high.

Wallflowers are in general hardy plants and very easy to care for; they grow in good garden soil and are easily propagated by seeds or cuttings.

# Chrysanthemum

The chrysanthemum particularly in horticulture is far from being definitely accepted. The name covers in fact not only the species making up the genus chrysanthemum of the botanists, but some similar plants from different families.

The name chrysanthemum (golden flower) comes from the characteristic golden-yellow color which most species had, at least in the primitive types. But cultivation has so modified this genus that the yellow color has completely disappeared in a great many varieties. As typical of real chrysanthemums, there is the old garden chrysanthemum which came from Mediterranean Europe, it is a perennial plant cultivated as an annual. One variety with completely white flowers was obtained which is very hardy and comes up in any position. Its very abundant flowers bloom successively from June until the frosts.

The most remarkable of all is the Indian chrysanthemum. This beautiful species has a considerable number of varieties, which differ in the size of the plant, the shape, sizes and color of the flowers and flowering season; among these are the common garden chrysanthemum with wide flowers and long spreading rays whose stems and flower-heads can reach enormous proportions, and the christmas flower, which is interesting because of the strange arrangement of its florets.

*Colchicum*

# Autumn crocus

The most well-known species is the autumn, fog or purple, crocus or common meadow saffron, called this because of the shape of the flower. It is also known as naked ladies because although the long, violet-pink flowers arising from the bulb immediately break through the earth and bloom in autumn, its leaves and fruits appear only during the following spring.

Every part of the plant gives off a strong sickening smell. The bulb, which contains a bitter acrid juice, is highly poisonous to man and animals.

*Convallaria*

# Lily-of-the-valley

These are perennial herbaceous plants with a creeping rootstock, with oval-lance-shaped leaves—few in number, often two—all radical and from the center of which arises a simple scape bearing clusters of flowers, a broadly bell-shaped perianth with six short tooth-like lobes curved outwards; six stamens are attached to the base of the perianth. There are very few species.

Common lily-of-the-valley is a small plant with white sweet-scented flowers that give way to scarlet berries. It is very widespread in Europe, found in woods and shady valleys where it flowers in springtime.

# Crocus

The crocus is a perennial plant with a rhizome made up of two superimposed corms covered with several tunics, from which arise long, straight almost linear leaves folded into a fascicule surrounded by a sheath. The flowers, borne on a short radical scape, have a large, colored funnel-shaped perianth with a slender elongated tube made up of six free segments alternating on two rows; there are three stamens in the throat of the perianth.

The crocus in its type of vegetation has some peculiarities worth noting. Often the leaves appear after the flowers and, at least in most species, appear very early in spring or even and at the end of the winter. The plants can often flower and go through all the stages of vegetation without being planted out. The crocus covers a great many species, but several are poorly defined. They generally grow in mountainous regions but most are cultivated in gardens as ornamental plants.

Generally regarded as originating in the East, but found spontaneously in the mountains of Southern Europe, the crocus seems to have been known since Antiquity —it was particularly abundant in Lebanon and Sicily. The Egyptians, Hebrews and Phoenicians used it for medicinal and culinary purposes; it was also used for perfumery.

The Sybarites consumed great quantities of it and the Romans used it often for making dyes. Saffron is obtained from the anthers of any two species.

# Cyclamen

This genus covers perennial plants with a rounded, flattened voluminous blackish tuber from which arise fibrous roots below and on the sides, and above, leaves with a long reddish petiole or leaf-stalk, with a spear-shaped, kidney-shaped or angular limb, often tinged with purple-red on the inner surface. The scapes, which also arise from the tuber and go beyond the petioles, each terminate in a reflexed flower, that has a calyx with five segments; a corolla with five petals standing up toward the sky and turned in on themselves, and five stamens; the fruit is a small rounded capsule. There are about fifteen species. Common cyclamen or sow-bread grows in the natural state in stony places. This tuber, which has so smell, but a bitter taste, is a very strong purgative. It was once highly recommended by doctors as such; it was also said to cure tumors, dropsy, scrofula, and chronic diseases. Since then, it has been mainly recommended for ornamental purposes. Its white-dappled leaves, and very elegantly shaped white, pink or purple flowers make an attractive show.

*Dahlia*

# Dahlia

Dahlias, which in autumn give a dash of color to the garden, were introduced into Europe in 1789 by a director of the Botanical Garden of Mexico. They bloomed for the first time in Spain in 1791. Less than a century later, many other countries had also adopted them.

Dahlias are generally large perennial plants, with a straight strong stalk, bearing opposite, deeply-toothed dark green leaves. The flowers are gathered into terminal capitulums, with a yellow disc surrounded by florets of varying shades. The most widespread species and also the earliest known is the common dahlia which came from Mexico like all the others. The roots are tuberous, fleshy and very fat. The stem is hollow, branched, growing sometimes to over 2 meters. The flowers or rather flower-heads, borne on long auxillary peduncles vary between 10 and 15 centimeters in diameter. But the typical dahlia, found today only in botanical gardens, can scarcely give an idea of the varieties obtained in our time. Colors have been varied in every possible permutation.

*Delphinium*

# Larkspur

The *delphinium* or dolphin-flower owes its name to the shape of the nectaries. These are herbaceous plants with variously denticulate leaves; the many-colored flowers grow in terminal clusters or panicles. Stavesacre or licebane, easily recognizable by its very short sac-like spur, yields delphinine, which is poisonous; the seeds are particularly poisonous.

*Dianthus*
# Pink

There are over a hundred species of pinks. Clove pink or carnation is the most well-known species; this is a perennial plant with solitary terminal red flowers in the standard. Originating in northern Africa, but cultivated for several centuries elsewhere, it has produced innumerable varieties with double or semi-double flowers—purple, white, yellow or variegated in various ways. The China or India pink is a biennial with a branched stem and solitary velvety-purple or white, purple-spotted flowers; there are many varieties with huge single or double flowers of pale violet, bright red marked with white, pure white variegated, etc. Feathered pink of Indian eye is a small perennial plant with very sweet-smelling pale pink, white or purplish spotted flowers.

## *Digitalis*
# Foxglove

These are plants with large flowers growing in terminal clusters or spikes; the calyx has five almost equal segments; the corolla has a long bell-shaped tube resembling the finger of a glove or a sewing thimble hence the many popular derivatives such as "fairy fingers" or "witches thimble."

These are about fourty species, the best-known being the common foxglove, also known as bloody finger or dead men's bells. A tall erect biennial, its flowers form a long slender unbranched spike, bright pinkish-purple in color, with purple spots on a white ground on the lower side of the corolla tube within. The important drug digitalin, which slows the heart and affects the whole circulation, is obtained from the leaves. The whole plant is poisonous.

Rusty foxglove is found in Southeast Europe; it grows over a meter high and has a long slender spike of almost globular, reddish-yellow flowers.

*Euphorbia*

# Spurge

The "flowers" of these plants are in reality compound; they are made up of several one-stamened male flowers and one-stalked female flowers, all encircled by a perianth-like involucre of four to five small teeth alternating with five or six swollen glands which are more or less half-moon-shaped.

Poisonous gum thistle has an erect fleshy stem between 1 and 2 meters high and as thick as an arm. Leaves are reduced to spines and the rather small flowers grow in solitary umbels. This plant is found in Africa and India and is cultivated in gardens. Cattemundoo or Callemundoo gum plant is similar in appearance but the ribs of the stem are more slender and the flowers grow in the intervals. This species is found on the coasts of Africa. These two species plus that found in the Canary Islands produce euphorbium, known in medecine as euphorbium gum.

Of the American species, ipecacuanha spurge has roots which can replace those of real ipecacuanha for medical purposes. The European species are mostly herbaceous with a straight stem sparsely covered with leaves terminating in an umbel; they are biennial or perennial. Sun spurge, also known as Saturday's pepper and devil's churnstaff, has a juice which causes extreme irritation if it gets near the eyes, the discomfort to the eye-lids lasting several days. *Euphorbia heterodoxa* is known for the production of alveloz milk, hailed as a cure for cancer.

# Gladiolus

These are plants of the iridaceae or iris family, with long flat sword-shaped leaves.

They are perennial plants, with a bulbous rhizome or root, from which arise long leaves with clearly marked longitudinal veins. The brightly-colored flowers have spathes and grow in one-sided terminal spikes; the perianth is composed of six more or less equal, free segments arranged somewhat asymmetrically and alternating in two rows.

The common sword-lily is very widespread and its pretty pink flowers make it stand out. It is sometimes used in gardens, above all for borders; but generally the following species are rightly preferred.

The Byzantine or large-flowered sword-lily is fairly like the common sword-lily, but is taller and the flowers are larger, more numerous and more brightly colored. The cardinal-flowered sword-lily which originates from the Cape of Good Hope owes its name to the scarlet of its flowers. The branching sword-lily is regarded as a hybrid of the two previous species.

*Heliotropium*

# Heliotrope

The characteristics of the heliotrope are as follows: a deeply five-lobed calyx; a bell or funnel-shaped five-lobed corolla, the lobes of which are separated by a longitudinal fold and often a small tooth, the throat without teeth, scales or hairs; the five stamens attached to the corolla; a very short terminal style; a peltate stigma.

The Peruvian heliotrope or cherry-pie has white or lilac flowers; they are very sweet smelling, somewhat similar to vanilla. In the summer, this plant has to be kept slightly sheltered in a southern exposure. It needs to be watered frequently. In winter it must be kept in temperate soil; it grows without difficulty in the house, provided it is watered from time to time. It can be grown from seeds or cuttings, in springtime and in summer.

The common heliotrope is found in abundance in sandy waste places and waysides; its stem is erect, branched and softly hairy; its flowers are white, arranged in forked spikes, completely unscented.

*Helleborus*

# Hellebore

The hellebore covers a dozen species which grow in temperate or northern regions. It seems to prefer dry stony uncultivated places, where it shines by its elegant habit and foliage. Flowers bloom in early spring and sometimes in the heart of winter. All these plants give off an unpleasant sickening smell; they have a bitter, acrid, burning taste.

Their medical properties, famous from antiquity, are generally very active but they vary according to the climate.

Bear's foot or black hellebore is a perennial plant, forming broad thickset clumps. From the middle of its palmate leaves, deeply cut into several lobes, arise naked scapes somes 0.30 m high at the most, ending in one or two large whitish-pink flowers, that come with the new leaves. This species, which is the prettiest of all, begins flowering toward the end of December—hence the common name of Christmas rose—and flowering continues throughout the winter.

*Hesperis*

# Dame's violet

The characteristics of this flower are a very short style, a deeply two-lobed stigma, with the lobes more or less erect and free, linear fruit, valves with distinct median and lateral veins. Flowers are pink, purple, yellow or white. They are herbaceous plants, annuals, biennials or perennials.

*Hyacinthus*
# Hyacinth

Hyacinth flowers are borne on a scape in a spike-like cluster. Each flower is bi-lobed and made up of a color bell-shaped perianth with a splayed limb, six stamens in the tube on the perianth, and short filaments; the three-celled ovary, each cell holding a small number of ovules, is surmounted by a short style ending in a stigma.

The common garden hyacinth has straight obtuse leaves shorter than the scape; the four to ten flowers form a lax, erect cluster. This plant has been considerably exploited, mainly in Holland; Harlem is the center of this trade. The Dutch are particularly careful, not to say meticulous, in the cultivation of hyacinths; committees have been set up to examine the new varieties and decide their value. Because of the infinite care taken in their cultivation and, it seems, because of the advantage of the climate, Holland today has a considerable number of varieties of hyacinth among which more than five hundred sufficiently characteristic to be easily distinguished one from the other.

The hyacinth is happy in a light soil and prefers a rather cold and damp climate.

*Ipomoea*

# Morning-glory

"Volubilis" is used to describe very long stems or branches which, not having the strength to support themselves, twine around the nearest body—convolvulus or bindweed is a familiar example. Some of these plants twine to the right, some to the left, but there is always one direction per species. Plants with twining stems or branches are called climbing plants.

The flowers of the ipomoea (American bindweed or morning-glory) sometimes very large and brilliantly colored, are borne on simple or branchy peduncles; they are similar in shape to bindweed. Several species are used in ornamental gardens, for example the scarlet-flowered bindweed or star glory originating in Latin America, or the common or red morning-glory. The Malabar gourd is the most beautiful species.

# Iris

There are about a hundred species of iris. They are perennial plants with a creeping rhizome or solid bulb, large bright flowers, often richly colored, sheathed in scaly spathes with a short perianth, three sometimes downy sepals, generally small erect petals, three stamens in the corolla and a style spread into three petaloid laminas. Sowings have considerably increased the varieties of some species. They are mainly reproduced by separating the rhizomes.

German or common iris, also known as flowering flag, is a multiflorous plant with smooth leaves shorter than the stem. Flowers are violet in color.

The Florentine iris or orris-root plant is a very similar species to the above, but is smaller with almost white flowers.

The yellow iris or water flag usually grows in marshes and streams. It has a strong, articulated horizontal rootstock, with a lot of small roots on it. The flowers, usually three or four on one stem, which sometimes grow over a meter high, are yellow. The rootstock of this species is bitter and purgative when fresh; its smell is almost imperceptible. Dried, it becomes red.

The other species are used as ornamental plants. Some examples are the dwarf iris, used for borders; the clouded iris or Spanish flag with many varieties; the morning iris from Asia Minor, whose white flowers streaked with violet make rather a pretty effect; the Siberian iris with blue and white hyacinth-scented flowers.

*Lilium*
# Lily

Lilies are found in most gardens. Few plants have such an interesting history; the lily has been appreciated by the horticulturist and the poet, who for all time made it the emblem of innocence and purity. It is frequently mentioned in the Bible.

The name Susan, borne by several women in the Old and New Testaments, comes from a Hebrew word meaning lily. The Greeks created lilies from Juno's milk.

A plant with a scaly bulb, a straight, simple stem, bearing alternate lance-shaped leaves, terminating in one or several large, fine flowers, the common white lily, also known as Juno's rose, grows to about one meter. The tiger lily from China has flowers the color of thin red lead with black spots; the Philadelphian martagon is orange red; the pomponian lily or little Turk's cap which grows mainly in the East, is a rich flame red. The gold-striped lily of Japan has very large, showy flowers.

The scent of the flowers, which fades on drying, is somewhat reminiscent of the hyacinth.

*Lilium martagon*

# Martagon lily

This plant has stems about a meter high, each bearing up to thirty flowers; these nodding flowers have segments rolled outwards in the form of a turban. Generally, the flowers are either reddish inside and purplish in color, with some black spots on the exterior, or they have a white background spotted with black. They smell unpleasant.

According to Greek mythology, Apollo involuntarily killed young Hyacinthus with a discus and changed him into a flower of that name; it is agreed today that the hyacinth *(hyacinthus)* of the Ancients was really the martagon lily.

The bulbs of this beautiful plant are particularly widespread in Russia between the Volga and the Urals and, grown today in most gardens, they long served to feed the Baskir peoples.

The Canadian martagon lily, with an erect violet-tinged stem sometimes more than 2 m high, bears medium-sized reflexed flowers which are bright-orange spotted with brown-purple; thirty of fourty of them are clustered into one magnificent pyramidal panicle.

*Linaria*
# Toadflax

These were long confused with antirrhinum, but differ in that the corolla here is prolonged into a long spur at the base.

Common toadflax or butter-and-eggs is a perennial plant growing to about 0.50 m; its leaves are glaucous. Before flowering, this plant resembles some species of spurge, but the white juice of the latter, irritant and poisonous, is enough to distinguish between them. The flowers grow in terminal spikes; they are large, sulphur-yellow, with an orange throat-boss. They sometimes seem to have small black spots at the base which are in fact holes made by the bees to reach the nectar, since they could not do so through the throat of the corolla.

It has served many uses, medicinal and cosmetic over the years. In the sixteenth century Jerome Wolf, director of the College of Augsburg, prepared an unguent from the flowers to treat skin diseases and one Guillaume de Hesse bought the secret from him at the price of a fat ox each year for the rest of his life.

# Lobelia

All the lobelias have a milky, acrid caustic and even poisonous juice. The most dangerous in this respect is the variety found in Jamaica, with a stem of over 0.32 m high, whose white flowers have a tube 0.10 m long. People rarely go near it since it is said that a very small quantity of its sap on the skin is enough to open sores immediately that are very difficult to heal. Acrid lobelia, widespread in Europe, is cultivated for its beautiful blue flowers. These are clustered on a terminal raceme: the juice of this plant is also very dangerous, hence its name. The brilliant lobelia, with scarlet flowers, originated in Mexico.

The cardinal-flower lobelia is the one most cultivated. It is covered in down and has a simple straight stem about 1 meter high; its oval leaves are acute at both ends; it has large scarlet flowers. They often seem to be unilateral plants because of their reaction to light, which draws the flowers to one side. This species is perennial; it grows in abundance in damp parts of the United States particularly in Virginia.

The tall blue lobelia, originating in the northern forests of America, grows to about 0.50 m high; its leaves are acute, irregularly toothed; the flowers are blue and tinged with violet on the tube, growing in a terminal cluster. When rubbed between the hands it gives off a noxious smell.

*Lupinus*
# Lupin

Although the lupin looks like a fairly modest plant, few others can boast as interesting a history. Its reputation goes back a very long way, and it is frequently mentioned by the authors of Antiquity. The Greeks, who received it from the Egyptians, cultivated it wholesale for fodder mixer with straw. Theophrastes recommends it for this purpose. Its seeds were used for food. The philosophers and particularly the Cynics made it the basis of their diet and used to carry it about with them.

Lupins are characterized by palmate leaves with five to eleven leaflets; their fairly large flowers grow in terminal clusters. There are a great many species which mostly grow in the temperate regions of the world, particularly in North America.

The white lupine is the most interesting species. Its straight stem, which grows to 0.50 m, bears palmate leaves with five or seven oblong-oval leaflets, smooth above and silky hairy below, ending in a terminal spike of white flowers. It is an annual regarded as originating in the Levant.

This plant is quite common in flowerbeds. It is a kind of natural clock because it is always turned toward the sun, following the movement even when this planet is not to be seen or is momentarily hidden behind clouds. Every evening when the sun is on the horizon, the leaflets fold in two, longitudinally, bringing their edges close together; at the same time they bend toward their leaf-stalk and bow down toward the earth.

# Lychnis, campion

These are mostly perennial plants with opposite simple leaves; sepals are fused into a tubular calyx with five short tooth-like lobes; the fruit is a capsule with five teeth.

Chalcedonian or scarlet lychnis is also known as Bridget in her bravery, the cross of Jerusalem, the flower of Bristow or of Constantinople, and is easily recognizable by its stems and its downy yellowish-green leaves. It flowers all summer. Cultivation has produced saffron yellow, orangey and flame or white varieties and doubles.

Meadow lychnis or campion, known as ragged Robin or cuckoo flower, has blood-red flowers with the petals cut into deep lobes. It flowers in the height of summer.

*Matthiola*
# Stock

There are about thirty species of these plants, mostly herbaceous, which are all covered with branched hairs. The flowers grow in a terminal cluster.

Brompton stock or „Hopes" is a robust perennial with white woolly leaves; varieties are white, pink, red, or violet, in singles, doubles or even proliferous. The flowers are faintly scented and go on appearing for months. It is a beautiful plant and very easy to grow.

Ten-week stock is smaller than the above but is similar in the woolliness of its leaves and the color and scent of the flowers. The double varieties are particularly popular.

*Mimulus*
# Monkey-flower

These are herbaceous plants with large, richly colored, solitary flowers. They are sometimes called bastard foxglove.

Yellow monkey-flower is the most widespread species. The large yellow flowers have red spots in the throat. The musk plant has smaller flowers with no red spots and as its name suggests, has a musky scent. Another fine specimen is the cardinal or scarlet monkey-flower. All these plants grow particularly on the west coast of the Americas, from California to Chile.

*Myosotis*

# Forget-me-not

Forget-me-nots cover about fifty herbaceous species, generally small, and almost all originating from the Old World; they are all closely covered with hairs; their leaves are petiolary at the bottom of the stem, and sessile at the top. Their small, often graceful, flowers are a pretty azure-blue, sometimes white or pinkish, with the throat of the corolla tinged with yellow to a greater or lesser extent. Inflorescence catches the eye because it is rolled into the shape of a scorpion's tail, hence its other name, scorpion grass.

*Narcissus*

# Daffodil

The root of this plant is a tunic bulb; the leaves are radical along the length of the stem, linear flat or channelled; the terminal flowers are either solitary or clustered in umbels; they are never straight but slightly inclined; the ovary and calyx are adherent and surmounted by a simple style.

A great many varieties are used as ornamental plants in the gardens; their graceful habit, delicate perfume, and beautiful colors are the notable characteristics of this family, with various shades from snow-white or golden-yellow to orange or purple. They have been grown from very early times.

Most multiflorous species, species with clusters or umbels, originate in southern countries; they are very sensitive to cold. Flowering is retarded by drought.

*Nicotiana*

# Tobacco

These are herbaceous plants generally with full leaves; the flowers, growing in terminal clusters or panicles, have a slightly irregular, persistent, bell-shaped five-lobed calyx; an elongated, funnel-shaped five-segment corolla; five stamens with long filaments. The many species of this genus grow in America particularly in the central parts of the continent; today many are cultivated extensively in almost all warm or temperate regions of the world.

*Nicotiana Tabacum* or large tobacco is an annual plant, glandular and hairy on all its herbaceous parts; its stem, which can be as long as 2 m or more, is straight, robust, branched at the top bearing large oval-heart-shaped shining leaves; the large pink or purple flowers grow in clusters. This species, originating in the hot regions of South America, has been the most commonly grown since ancient times, either in gardens for its graceful habit and beautiful flowers or in quantity in the fields for economic purposes. It has produced many varieties or races varying in vigor with leaves differing in length and width, acute, bright pink flowers or more or less dark pink flowers.

Maryland tobacco or large-leaved tobacco, regarded by most writers as a variety of the previous species, differs from *Nicotiana Tabacum* by stockier stems, fuller and more wavy leaves. Virginia tobacco is also connected by several botanists to the first species; its stem, which rarely grows higher than 1.50 m, bears smaller leaves obliquely pointed at the apex; its pinkish flowers grow in many clusters.

*Nymphaea*

# Water-lily

The white water-lily, variously known as bobbins or flatter dock, is a tall fine plant with a very long, fleshy, knotted rhizome, yellowish-brown on the outside, white within, with many fibrous roots below, and round, floating shiny leaves above; the large flowers, sometimes rich yellow, pure white or slightly pink, are solitary, fragrant and long-stalked.

This is a very common plant found in clear, still waters. To propagate it in ornamental lakes, it is enough to throw a few seeds or better, some bits of fresh rhizome in the water. It flowers from May to August and the rhizome should be picked preferably during the summer since it is stoutest at that time.

*Paeonia*

# Peony

There are more than twenty species of peony, among which is the common garden peony with its long fat tubers, brownish on the outside and whitish on the inside, and a strong, even sickening smell. The straight stem grows to between 0.50 m and 0.70 m. The leaves are smooth, soft green on the upper side and even softer green on the underside; the flowers are large and form one piece with the end of the main stem and the branches; cultivation gives doubles. In the variety commonly known as the male peony, the seed is red; in the female peony it is very dark blue; the two pistils are downy, as are the capsules which subsequently replace them. By cultivation, variegated peonies, and several double white, pink or crimson varieties have been obtained; the last variety is the most common. They can be planted outside where they remain several years.

The Chinese tree peony is an attractive shrub which grows to one meter and over; in its native country it grows higher. The stem is cylindrical and smooth and it has lovely big pink or white terminal flowers; their scent is something like a rose. They have several layers of many petals.

# Poppy

Poppies are annual or perennial plants which secrete a white milky sap; their leaves are toothed in various ways. The large solitary flowers on the end of long peduncles have a calyx with two herbaceous concave sepals, a corolla with four opposite petals arranged in a cross, crumpled in the bud before the opening of the many stamens.

The carnation, paeony or opium poppy, typical of the genus, is a plant with a fusiform or spindle-shaped root; the stem, which often grows to 1 meter high, is cylindrical and erect.

The poppy came from the East and since very early times it has been celebrated in mythology and history (it was made the main attribute of Morpheus, god of sleep).

Garden poppies were early used as ornamental plants and are very important still today. There are innumerable varieties: single, double or proliferous flowers which are either with fringed or wavy petals plain or variegated, offering every shade of white, pink, scarlet, purple, violet, garnet red, corn-poppy red, ash grey, flax grey, etc.

The poppy needs a warm exposure and should be sheltered against high winds; it prefers light clayey-sandy soil or clayey-chalky soil with very permeable subsoil.

The white opium poppy is taller than the others—its capsules ovoid and bigger, and its seeds white, rarely tinged with purple. Cultivation is the same as for the others of the species.

*Pelargonium*

# Geranium

Geraniums are herbaceous plants with leaves placed opposite one another on the stem. The corolla of the flowers has five petals. There are a great many species. Herb robert or red shanks is easily recognizable because of its hairy, knotted and reddish stems. The Ancients, because of this characteristic feature, called the plant *ruberta* or *rubertiana* (from the Latin ruber or red). Hence by modification, come the names rupertiana and robertiana which make up the scientific name *geranium robertianum.* This plant, which is strong-smelling, indeed quite unpleasantly so, enjoyed a great reputation in ancient medicine. Today it has lost its cachet but is grown in gardens like other varieties for the beauty of its flowers. Endres's cranesbill is often used for round flowerbeds, its large pink flowers last all the year round. All these plants come up outdoors; any soil suits them provided it is light and sufficiently chalky.

# Petunia

Petunias originated in Latin America. They are particularly cultivated as annuals. Common white petunia is a glandular hairy plant which sometimes gives off a fairly disagreeable smell particularly in the evening and when the weather is stormy. Its beautiful large, white, scented flowers bloom from May till the end of the autumn. Petunia violacea is more floriferous than the previous species—from which it differs above all by leaves varying in breadth and by smaller purple-violet flowers which are velvety and less scented. It has produced several varieties. "Petunias," writes Mr. de Vilmorin, "are without fear of contradiction the most delightful ornamental garden flowers. The infinite variety of their colours, the brightness, abundance and perfume of the flowers and at the same time the hardiness of the plants, which easily withstand drought and do well in any soil, rank petunias among the best outdoor species."

Left to their own devices, petunias grow into shrubby, very branchy clumps with the stalks spreading over the ground then straightening up, covered with gaily-colored flowers contrasting vividly with the foliage. The stems have a tendency to go on forever, as it were, and to become either recurved or almost climbing. They can be trained over trellises, balustrades or terraces. They are also suitable for rock-gardens and large urns.

# Phlox

Particularly widespread in North America, these are plants with simple leaves, the lower ones opposite, the higher ones alternate; the purple, violet, red, pink, blue or white flowers are very striking. Several species are cultivated in gardens, such as tall garden phlox or blossom withy; Texan pride, and Carolina phlox. Several varieties have sweet-scented flowers.

All these plants can be used for borders, clumps and flowerbeds.

*Primula*
# Primrose, cowslip

The name of this flower brings to mind the first days of spring when the primroses or cowslips carpet the woods, meadows and gardens, catching the eye with their colors varying from white to red, from bright to pale yellow, from velvety purple to brown.

The characteristic features are a five-toothed slightly hairy calyx, a regular corolla, cylindrical, five stamens included, borne on very short filaments. Flowering begins in early March and lasts with some renewals for a month to six weeks; when there is a fine autumn it begins again. There are some sixty species, one of the best-known being the cowslip. Its yellow sweet-scented flowers can be used to make home-made wine and it has been an important medicinal plant in the past. Bear's ear or auricula is sought after for its very sweet-scented flowers; a strong plant, it has vivid corollas varying in shade from crimson, violet brown and olive-green to yellow, offering every imaginable variegation.

The Chinese primrose is a perennial; its stem is non-existent or very stunted, with wavy-edged viscous hairy leaves of a cheerful green, sometimes slightly reddish on the underside; amid the leaves arise scapes 0.15 to 0.30 m long, terminating in elegant panicles with large slightly scented pretty pink flowers, yellowish at the throat. This species has produced many varieties with white, salmon-pinkish, rust-colored, variegated single or double flowers, with entire or fringed edges. The plant flowers all the year round.

*Pulsatilla*

# Anemone, pasque flower

The anemone, dane-flower or pasque flower, is a fairly common pretty plant. It is found in woods, on the grass of dry open hillsides, where it flowers from March to May, and many people cultivate it in their gardens.

It has petiolate leaves, a large flower which is erect or slightly nodding, whose perianth, which is pure violet and tinged with lilac, is made up of six sepals.

*Ranunculus*

# Buttercup, crowfoot

These are herbaceous plants with yellow or white flowers, occasionally purple, with a calyx which has five segments, a corolla with five petals and many stamens. There are a great many species spread throughout almost all the regions of the world but most particularly in the northern hemisphere.

They are more or less bitter-tasting, acrid and odorless. If chewed when freshly picked, they produce blisters on the lips and in the mouth that soon develop into gangrenous little sores. If swallowed, they cause inflammation in the digestive system. They are, in short, highly poisonous; the juice of some species applied to open wounds can, or so it is said, cause death.

Bulbous-rooted crowfoot or buttercup is very common throughout Europe and North America. The variety known as batchelor's buttons is a perennial noted for its bright yellow flowers. Asiatic crowfoot or common garden *ranunculus* is a plant with deeply toothed leaves, in the midst of which arises a stem some 0.25 m long on the average, terminating in a single large flower varying from white through every shade to purple.

*Salvia*

# Sage

Originating from southern Europe, this plant has been grown in gardens from time immemorial. The small-leaved varieties are the most delicate. It is more hardy in mediocre soil and it prefers a southern exposure.

The leaves of common garden sage are very aromatic, penetrating but pleasant; the taste is warm, spicy, bitter, slightly acrid and aromatic. They contain an essential oil made up of a mixture of two essences used by perfumers. The ancients used this plant for embalming. It can replace hops in beer-making.

Annual clary or red-topped sage is a plant with a stem of 0.35 m on the average with oblong-oval leaves covered with erect whitish hairs; the blue-violet purplish or white flowers with large bracts (of the same color) grow in false verticils which together make a long spike. It grows in southern regions and favors dry places. It is hardly grown except in botanical gardens; it could be used to advantage in landscape parks and gardens since all its varieties produce a good effect in clumps, round flowerbeds or borders. It needs a warm exposure, light soil and has to be watered a few times in summer. Annual clary, hardly used today, has similar but less active properties to common garden sage; this is also true for wild or meadow clary, a perennial plant with stems growing to between 0.30 m and 0.80 m high, bearing double-toothed or lobed leaves. The flowers of this species are blue, more rarely pinkish-blue or white, growing in spikes; they have a viscous calyx with a long corolla.

*Scabiosa*

# Scabious

These are herbaceous plants with opposite simple leaves. The scales of the receptacle are linear-lance-shaped and the involucre ends in a papery pleated cup; the calyx has five spreading stiff bristles.

Field scabious or lady's cushion is a perennial with a short rhizome; its branchy stems covered with stiff hairs grow to about 0.50 m. It grows almost anywhere but prefers a light substantial soil.

Scabious was formerly used to treat all manner of ailments, from pleurisy and persistent coughs to the plague and syphilis not to mention leprosy and other skin diseases. It is still used as a depurative.

Mournful widow or sweet scabious is an annual or biennial; its branchy stems grow to about 0.50 m high and bear toothed leaves; its flattened flower-heads are lilac-red violet or dark purple. There are single or double varieties, white, copper-pink and purple-flowered varieties and dwarfs with these colorings. This plant does well anywhere but originating from southern Europe it prefers a light soil and a warm airy position.

*Stachys*

# Woundwort

Woundwort is a hairy, downy, silky plant. It has a five-lobed calyx and a two-lipped corolla; the upper lip flat or arched, the lower lip three-lobed; the slender graceful stem bears purple-tinged flowers during the summer; the stem is erect, simple and grows to between 0.30 m to 0.40 m; lower leaves are oblong, shallow-toothed; the upper leaves are straighter.

The main species is betony. The flowers have a faint scent; the leaves are acrid and almost scentless; the root, which has an unpleasant taste, is a purgative. Taken as snuff, betony brings out the mucous membrane from the nostrils.

Other species are grown in gardens, for example the large-flowered betony, which originated in Siberia, it is a perennial. The stem is hairy, the many-toothed long heart-shaped leaves even more so; it has beautiful, big pink flowers.

*Strelizia*

# Bird of paradise flower

Also called bird's-tongue-flower, this is a large perennial plant with very large leaves on long stalks, with big brightly-colored flowers; the perianth has six segments alternating over two rows, the three outside being very bright orangey-yellow and those inside a beautiful blue.

These plants originate in the Cape of Good Hope.

*Thymus*

# Thyme

This little plant grows in abundance in woods and on lawns that catch the sun, and is found in many gardens.

Its stem, a little woody at the base, is divided into a large number of branches lying along the ground; it is erect near the apex and covered with small opposite oval leaves which are narrow at their base; flowers are purplish, and the corolla is longer than the calyx.

It is bitter tasting; but its aromatic smell explains its use as an herb in cooking.

*Tropoelum*

# Nasturtium

For a long time regarded as belonging to the geranium family, the genus nasturtium has become part of the tropaeolaceae. There are over thirty species which, in the beginning, grew throughout the Americas. The most famous is the tuberous-rooted nasturtium, a superb climbing plant that came from Peru.

Its stems, that rise several meters high, bear large shield-shaped blue-green leaves, and flowers of a characteristic color and shape with which everyone is familiar. All the parts of this plant taste similar to cress; indeed it has been called "Indian cress." Its flowers can garnish a salad and its young buds and immature seeds pickled in vinegar become capers.

The dwarf nasturtium, smaller than the above in every way, is also fairly common. Several species have tuberous rhizomes.

It was the flowers of a nasturtium that made the daughter of a scientist (who thought fit to mention it) think she saw flashes coming from it, an illusion doubtless caused by the brilliance of the flower—and the tired eyes of that young person.

*Tulipa*

# Tulip

Tulip are bulbous plants with oblong, oval or lance-shaped leaves; from the middle of these leaves arises a straight scape terminating in a solitary flower with six segments alternating over two rows. Several species have been cultivated as garden flowers since time immemorial; one in particular enjoyed a tremendous reputation and its cultivation became a fairly large branch of industry: Gesner's or common tulip. It grows to 0.25 m high on the average. The flowers are every possible shade except pure blue.

Originating of the East it was probably appreciated by the Greeks and Romans. Described for the first time by Conrad Gesner in 1559 on specimens grown from bulbs brought from Constantinople, it was propagated shortly afterwards in the Netherlands. Scarcely had it become known in that country when it was feted with extraordinary enthusiasm; the numbers of "mad tulip-growers" swelled from day to day. Tulips were even quoted on the Harlem stock exchange and some bulbs became incredibly valuable. The Admiral Lieskens was worth more than 4,000 florins; the Semper Augustus 2,000 florins. One day there were only two of the latter left. Someone offers 4,600 florins and a carriage-and-pair for one and a dozen acres of land for the other, but without success.

There are thousands of varieties of the common tulip, but only a few hundred selected ones are grown in gardens: these divide into singles and doubles subdividing in turn into early and late varieties.

*Verbena*

# Vervain

The numerous species of this plant are particularly widespread in the warm regions of the two continents; only one grows spontaneously in Europe; several others are cultivated in gardens.

Common vervain is a perennial plant with a spindle-shaped root; the stem, 0.50 m high on the average is stiff, erect or rising with branches bearing oval or oblong leaves, opposite, often deeply toothed; it has tiny lilac-blue flowers in elongated slender, terminal spikes. This completely scentless plant has a slightly bitter taste; it contains an astringent ingredient of a special type: placed on the skin it makes it bright red, which formerly earned it a reputation for being able to draw blood.

Vervain has been very famous from earliest times. The Druids venerated it in the same way as sacred mistletoe. It was gathered with superstitious ceremony: first the earth had to be offered an expiatory sacrifice, consisting of fruits and honey, then at the beginning of the dog days at dawn when neither the sun nor the moon was visible on the horizon, a circle was described around the plant which was then pulled up by the left hand.

Vervain thus obtained had wonderful properties, calmed fevers and other illnesses, was an antidote for poisonous snake-bites; destroyed spells, was a kind of charm for reconciling friends at variance and dispelling hatred. Strewn over guests at a banquet, it inspired gentle gaiety in them. Vervain was also highly thought of by the Greeks and Romans who called it holy herb. It was used to purify the altars of Jupiter and decorate them during sacrifices. Tufts of vervain dipped in lustral water were used to sprinkle houses in order to drive out evil spirits.

*Veronica*

# Speedwell, cancerwort

The flowers, usually blue, occasionally white or pinkish, grow in a terminal spike or cluster, or in lateral spikes borne in the axils of leafy bracts. The corolla has a very short tube and four wide-spreading, rounded and somewhat unequal lobes—the upper lobe is the largest, the lower the smallest.

Common speedwell, sometimes called medicinal tea speedwell, is a creeping rooting hairy perennial. It is a bitter and astringent plant used in herbal remedies. It contains a little tannin.

Spiked speedwell grows to about 0.20 or 0.30 m. Its flowers, very numerous, grow in a dense, long, cylindrical, terminal spike. They are usually bright blue. It is particularly usefull for gardens and parks, sloping ground, rocky, uneven or open places otherwise unsuitable for cultivation.

*Viola hybrida*

# Violet

The scented violet has been sung by poets as the emblem of modesty since time began. This is the species to which everything said or written about the violet, generally speaking, is related. It has been mentioned or described since Antiquity, although other plants have been confused with it.

The Greeks and Celts used it to decorate the nuptial couch of the bride and the coffin of maidens, a custom that was long preserved in Germany. The Athenians covered their heads with it for festivals thinking it prevented drunkenness.

The scented violet is a perennial plant with a creeping, knotted whitish rhizome with many fibrous hairy radicles. The flowers with which everyone is familiar, usually have the characteristic color which gives them their name however, occasionally they are purple-blue or even off-white. They are very sweet-smelling. This is a very widespread plant growing in woods, hedges, shrubs, grassy or shady places and in cultivated gardens.

It has produced a fair number of varieties with single or double flowers varying in size. *Viola odorata* (var.) *semperflorens* differs from the dog or hedge violet by a slightly larger and more scented flower but particularly because it flowers several times a year, from September and in the springtime to April; sometimes it also flowers in summer in cool, shady positions.

The Parma violet has small shiny bright; green leaves-large, broad, very full flowers of pale greyish or very pale blue, with a little white at the bottom.

These flowers have a very pleasant smell quite different from other violets. It is a fairly delicate variety.

The common violet flowers very early, often from February onwards. Because of this together with its sweet scent and the hardiness of the plant and the ease with which it can be grown and propagated, it is extremely popular with gardeners.

*Viola tricolor*

# Pansy

This plant very often varies greatly in the shape of its leaves, in the size and color of its flowers, according to where it grows, and horticulturists have modified it to an almost infinite degree. The two main varieties are the wild pansy and the cultivated pansy. The wild pansy, variously known as heart's ease, or jump-up-and-kiss-me, is an annual plant with a stem of 0.5 m long, it is angular, very smooth, branchy, diffuse, and bears oval crenelated leaves; the fairly small yellow flowers often spotted with violet, are set on long single axillary peduncles; the corolla is irregular and some stamens are fused with the anthers. This plant has almost no smell, but is bitter-tasting and slightly salty. It contains albumine and gum, a bitter extract, and one particular constituent, violine similar to emetine.

The garden pansy, regarded as a variety or race of the previous species can be distinguished from it in particular by its petals, which are much longer than the calyx, by its much larger flowers, which have much brighter and more varied colors. It is one of the best-loved ornamental plants. It has produced a great many varieties, as remarkable for their elegance and strangeness of their shape as for the richness of their colors. Those particularly well thought of are those have large, rounded flowers with bright contrasting colors and a mask in the middle. The pansy is very easily grown from seeds, gathered when the plant has reached maturity.

# Adam's needle, bear grass

These are perennial plants with underground or shrubby stems, straight, thick narrow leaves, often toothed and spiny, growing very close together in a fascicle or bundle. The flowers, growing on a long straight scape, have the characteristics usually associated with the liliaceae. There are about thirty species which grow particularly in the temperate and warm parts of America, several of which are cultivated in Europe.

The common Adam's needle or mound lily, has a great many roots, and a stem 0.3 to 0.4 m high. It is superb when in flower. It is used for hedges which, as long as there are no holes, form an effective and, at the same time, a pretty barrier. In landscape gardens they stand out even without their flowers because of the arrangement of the leaves. These plants can withstand very hard frosts and especially damp. The dagger plant or Spanish bayonet has a stem several meters high and narrow crenelated leaves; its flowers are white tinged with violet. Originating in the warm parts of North America and particularly widespread in California, it is more sensitive to frost then the previous one. Adam's needle and thread has many leaves, narrow at the base, noted for the grayish membrane which stands away from the edge in long silky filaments. The scape, 2 meters high, the lower part naked, ends in a superb pyramidal panicle of profuse greenish-white flowers larger than in the above-mentioned species. Soap-plant is another fine species with short stems and elongated, glaucous, fringed leaves; the long scape bears, in autumn, an ample panicle of short, rounded, white flowers, tinged red on the outside.

*Zinnia*

# Youth and Old Age

These are annual herbaceous plants, with opposite entire veined leaves, yellow and red flowers growing in large radial flowerheads. A dozen species are known growing in the central and warm regions of America. The most noted is the blood marigold or old maid's pink; this plant, with a stem that grows a meter high, flourishes in Mexico; it has produced many varieties with single or double flowers, with every shade from white to purple-red. It grows in the open air and often does its own sowing, and propagation offers no difficulty. Multiflorous zinnia is also cultivated; its stems are shorter than the above and the flowers are dull red and yellow in one variety.

Zinnias are very attractive ornamental plants because of their elegant habit and the varied colors and long flowering period. They are used for flowerbeds, making clumps, particularly in large gardens where very hardy elements are needed to withstand drought if need be. As cut flowers, they are perfect for bouquets.